HOW TO USE THIS BOOKLET

The information in this booklet is organized in two parts.

PART 1 GENERAL INFORMATION covers items of interest or things that you can see from all ferries.

PART 2 ROUTE INFORMATION gives a point-by-point description of highlights along each ferry route to Vancouver Island always starting from the mainland and going to the Island.

INDEX

MEET THE FLEETS

BRITISH COLUMBIA FERRIES: 24 blue and white ferries of the DOGWOOD FLEET serve the BRITISH COLUMBIA coast.

The 200 car and 1200 passenger QUEEN of VICTORIA is typical of the stretched ferries running the major routes (in background)., The smaller QUEEN of SIDNEY (foreground) plies the major Gulf Island routes.

Numerous smaller ferries like the PENDER QUEEN (left) holding 35-90 cars run between the Gulf Islands.

The QUEEN OF PRINCE RUPERT plying the northern coastal route carries 90 cars and 430 passengers. It is especially designed for open ocean travel and has a unique tilting bow for front end loading.

CANADIAN PACIFIC FERRIES. The PRINCESS of VANCOUVER carrying 90 cars runs directly from downtown Vancouver to downtown Nanaimo. It is similar to the PRINCESS MARGUERITE of the Seattle - Victoria run.

WASHINGTON STATE FERRIES operate two ferries, the EVERGREEN STATE and the WALLA WALLA through the picturesque San Juan Islands from Anacortes to Sidney.

BLACK BALL FERRIES. The COHO carrying 90 cars makes the daily run from Port Angeles to downtown Victoria.

NAVIGATIONAL AIDS

On the rocks was not a term invented by lovers of iced drinks.

In order to minimize the dangers of running aground man has devised various forms of markers and warning devices.

CHANNEL MARKERS

narrow channels are marked by buoys. The port or left side of a channel is indicated by black can buoys, the starboard or right side by red painted conical buoys or red spars.

BELL BUOYS

a bell mounted in a cage on a floating drum is often anchored to hazardous underwater rocks. Wave action sets the drum bobbing and the bell tolling.

LIGHTHOUSES

may be large or small, manned or unmanned, or the light may be fixed or flashing. Each light has a different flashing time so that the navigator can 'read the light'.
Fl. 19 sec. 57 ft. 19M means the light flashes every 19 seconds in a light 57 feet high and visible for 19 miles.
Gp Fl. (3) 12 sec. 19 ft. (U) means the light is seen as a group of three flashes every 12 seconds and is unmanned.

FOGHORNS

are often placed with lighthouses so that when fog obliterates the light the horn is still audible. A foghorn's deep, far-carrying, 'Beee-o' sound has only one meaning - "keep off".

TIDES AND CURRENTS

the rise and fall of the tide is caused by the gravitational pull of the sun and moon — the latter pulling 2 1/4 times as hard as the former. The greatest tides or spring tides occur when the sun, moon and earth are in line. The lesser seasonal tides or neap tides occur when the sun and moon are at right angles. The currents or water movements resulting from the changing tides are quite severe in many of the Gulf Island areas, often reaching 5-7 knots.

THE FLOW AND EBB OR FLOOD

the flood tide is the incoming or rising tide. The ebb tide is an outflowing tide.

TIDAL LINES

indicate where two water masses meet but don't really mix. The brown muddy summer runoff of the Fraser River fans out for 20-30 miles with noticeable tide lines separating each successive layer of brown fresh water.

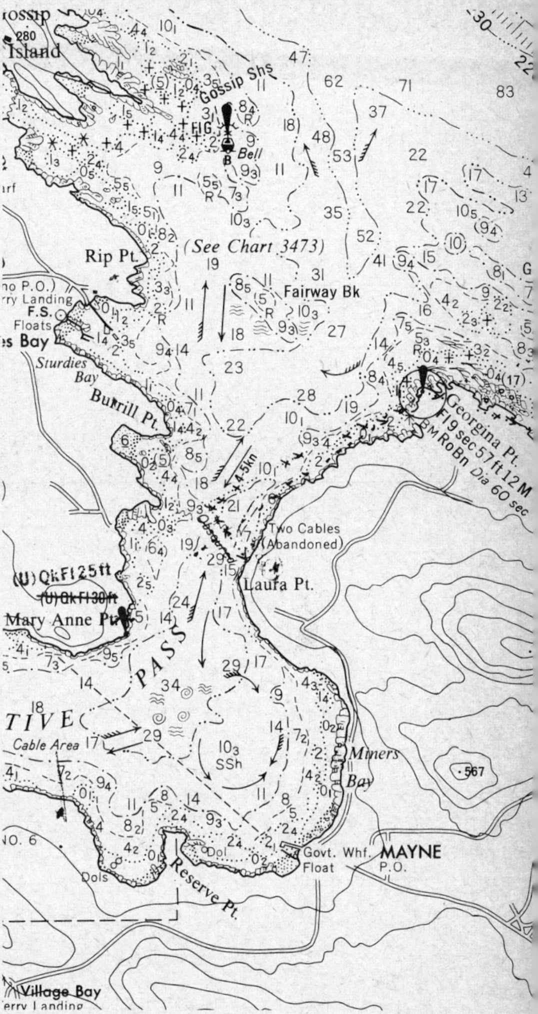

HYDROGRAPHIC CHART showing navigation aids: lights, depth, currents, etc. at entrance to Active Pass

SS PRINCESS MAY made a spectacular grounding in 1910 but all passengers escaped and the vessel was refloated with minimal damage.

MARINE MISCELLANEA

CONTRARY TO THE ACTIONS OF THE GULLS
THE POOP DECK IS NOT AN OUTDOOR BIFFY.

FLAGS

every vessel flys the flag of its country off the stern. When a vessel enters foreign waters it raises that country's flag midship.

SPEED OF A SHIP

is measured in knots - a horizontal measurement equal to 6076.1 feet. Therefore 1 nautical mile equals 1.15 statute miles.

FATHOMS

a unit for measuring depth in the sea where 6 feet equal 1 fathom.

CATS PAWS

are batches of wind rippled water in an otherwise calm glassy sea.

FLOTSAM

is a material thrown from a sinking boat that floats

JETSAM

is a discarded material from a sinking boat that sinks.

GARBAGE or LITTER is that which is thrown from a safely but carelessly operated vessel - Don't you be a Litter Bug

BEAUFORT SCALE

A scale of wind velocities employed in meteorological work. The wind velocity is measured by its pressure on a disk one square foot in area at a height of 33 feet in the open.

DESCRIPTION SPEED MPH.

CODE NO.	DESCRIPTION	SPEED MPH.	
0	CALM	LESS THAN 1	
1	LIGHT	1-3	
2	LIGHT BREEZE	4-7	
3	GENTLE BREEZE	8-12	
4	MODERATE BREEZE	13-18	WHITE CAPS
5	FRESH BREEZE	19-24	
6	STRONG BREEZE	25-31	
7	MODERATE GALE	32-38	
8	FRESH GALE	39-46	
9	STRONG GALE	47-54	CORMORANTS FLY BACKWARD
10	WHOLE GALE	54-63	PASSENGERS SEASICK
11	STORM GALE	64-75	FERRIES DON'T RUN.
12	HURRICANE	ABOVE 75	

CANADIAN
FLAG

FLAG OF THE PROVINCE
OF BRITISH COLUMBIA

BRITISH COLUMBIA FERRIES
FLAG

BRITISH COLUMBIA FERRIES
CAP CREST

CAPTAIN'S CAP

PROVINCIAL
COAT OF ARMS

officers insignia aboard this ship

MASTER,
CHIEF ENGINEER

CHIEF OFFICER,
or 2nd ENGINEER

2nd OFFICER,
or 3rd ENGINEER

JUNIOR
ENGINEER

CHIEF
STEWARD

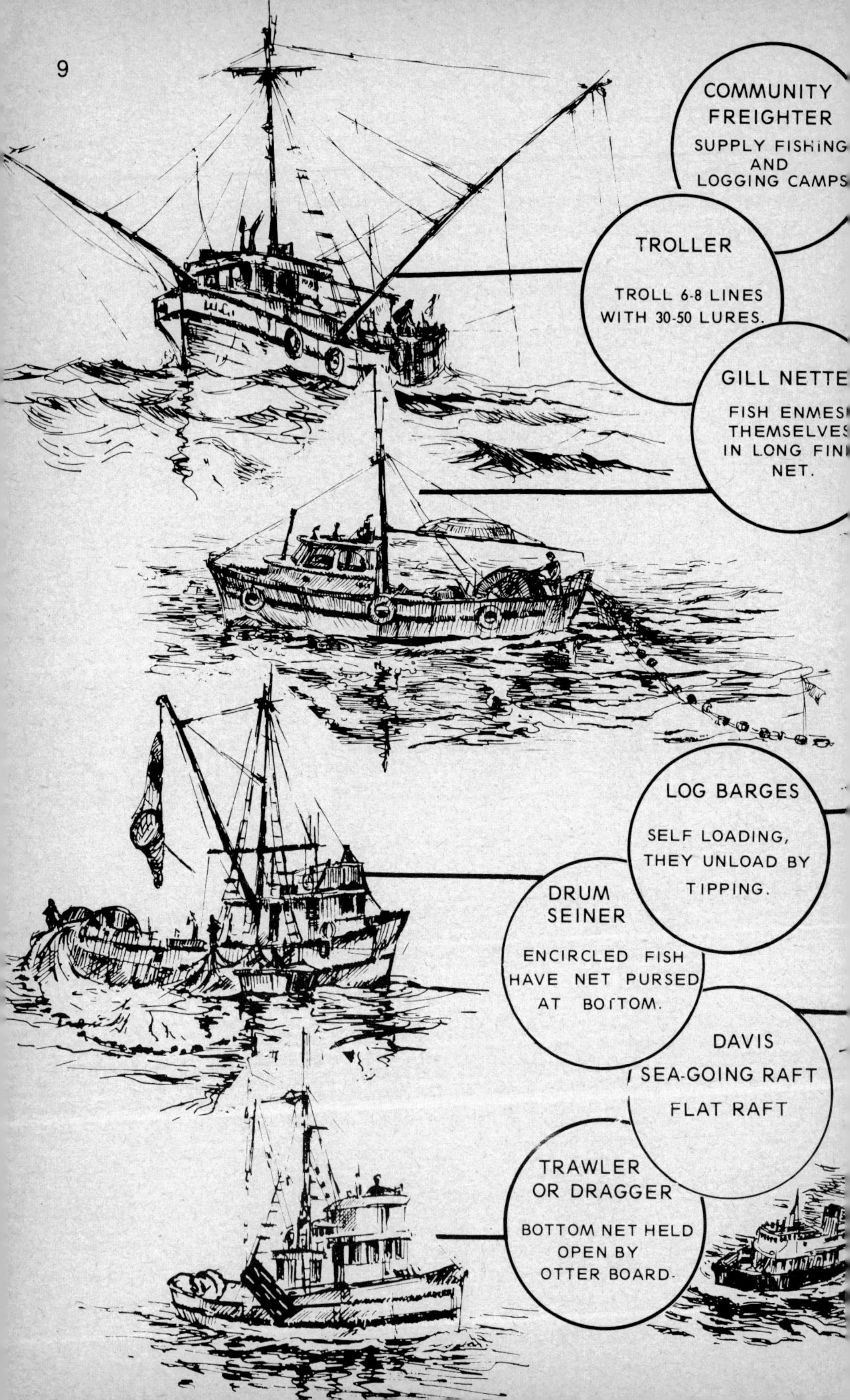
COMMUNITY FREIGHTER
SUPPLY FISHING AND LOGGING CAMPS
TROLLER
TROLL 6-8 LINES WITH 30-50 LURES.
GILL NETTE
FISH ENMES THEMSELVES IN LONG FIN NET.
LOG BARGES
SELF LOADING, THEY UNLOAD BY TIPPING.
DRUM SEINER
ENCIRCLED FISH HAVE NET PURSED AT BOTTOM.
DAVIS
SEA-GOING RAFT
FLAT RAFT
TRAWLER OR DRAGGER
BOTTOM NET HELD OPEN BY OTTER BOARD.

NTAINERIZED
FREIGHTER
MINIMIZES FREIGHT HANDLING.

OIL TANKER
THE COAST'S BIGGEST THREAT TO POLLUTION.

TRAIN BARGE
MOST GOING TO VANCOUVER IS. OR ALASKA

GENERAL
CARGO
BARGES

WILDLIFE

The inside waters of British Columbia and Washington, are extremely rich in invertebrates, fish, birds and mammals. A few of the dominant and common species are illustrated here.

STELLARS SEA LIONS 1000-2400 lb. brown animals related to trained seal's of circus. Occasionally they are seen 'porposing' in turbulent waters where they play and hunt for course fish.

HARBOR SEALS 200-400 lb- white to black with spots. Most commonly seen around docks with just head protruding from water or sunning on rocks.

KILLER WHALES are more common in inside waters than anywhere else in world. There is no record of them killing man. They eat dogfish sharks and seals. Bulls have longest dorsal fins. Usually travel in family groups. Size: 12-25 feet.

FISHES AND SUCH

Our nutrient rich waters team with plankton which in turn feeds many fishes and invertebrates.

SALMON yes, even from the ferry salmon can occasionally be seen finning and jumping. (see page 46 for 5 species).

HERRING BALL When HERRING or SANDLANCE, small bait fish, are driven to the surface by larger fish hundreds of gulls and eagles will be seen diving for the easy meal.

DOCKSIDE In the waters below the ferry dock the commonly seen fish are SEA PERCH, a species that give birth to live young. Size: 2 - 12".

Occasionally ROCK FISH and LING COD can be seen around pilings chasing schools of small fish.

PILING LIFE Thick encrustations of blue/black MUSSELS cling to most pilings. They are all edible if the water is not polluted and sell for about $4.00 per pound in the gourmet food market. The white encrustations above the darker mussels are BARNACLES which like the mussels filter plankton from the water with frilly hands.

STARFISH The five rayed ORANGE and PURPLE STARS and the larger orange to grey SUNFLOWER STAR frequent pilings to eat mussels.

BALD EAGLES

The Bald Eagle is the emblem of the United states, yet it is an endangered species.
Fortunately the B.C. coast still supports over 12,000 pairs. In the Canadian Gulf Islands 97 pairs annually raise young while in the adjacent U.S. San Juan Islands only 1 or 2 pairs raise young.

ADULTS can live 50 years. It takes 4-6 years to get the white head and tail.

YOUNG are in nest April to July. (see Tsawwassen-Swartz Bay route for more)

NESTS are always near water; occasionally conspicuous from ferry. Can be 8-12 ft. across and hold 6-8 people.

PERCHES are marked on route maps. Look for white heads.

FOOD mainly fish caught live or scavenged on beach.

Fourteen species pass along our coast but only four are commonly seen from ferry.

GLAUCOUS-WINGED
HERRING
MEW
BONAPARTE'S

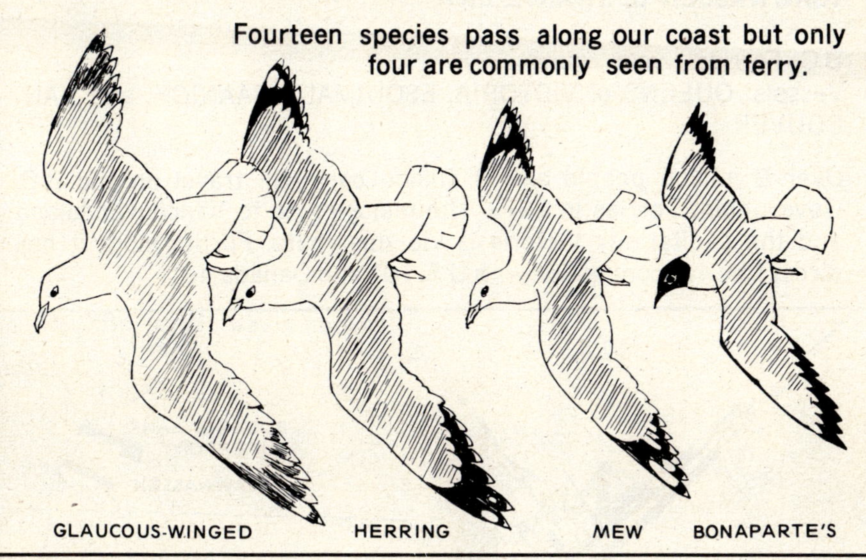

MISCELLANEOUS BIRDS

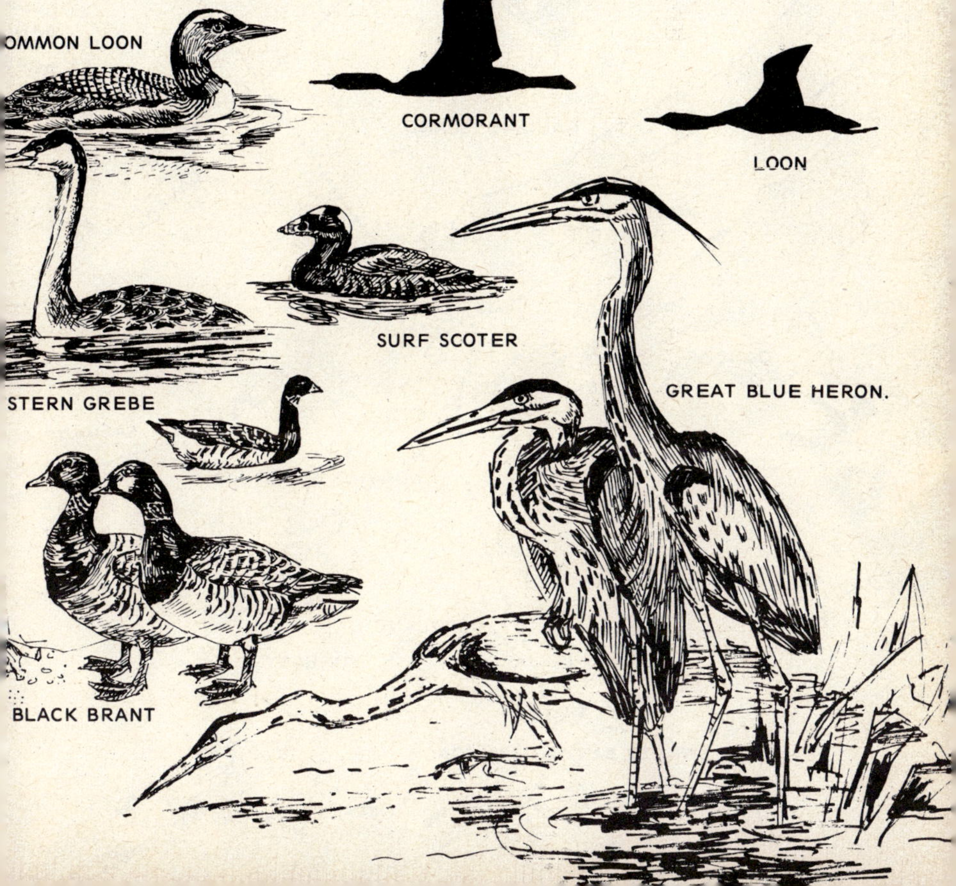

OMMON LOON
CORMORANT
LOON
SURF SCOTER
STERN GREBE
GREAT BLUE HERON.
BLACK BRANT

TSAWWASSEN to SWARTZ BAY

B.C. Ferries - year round
Vessels: QUEENS of VICTORIA, ESQUIMALT, SAANICH, and VAN-
COUVER.

Over 8 million people and 3 million cars will travel on the B.C.
Government Ferries in 1973. The major route to Vancouver Island
and the capital city Victoria is via this route. Furthermore it has
direct freeway connection with U.S. 101 and Canada 401.

TSAWWASSEN TERMINAL

Opened 9 June, 1960 only 23 months after B.C. Government announced it was buying companies that did not wish to expand ferry service to Vancouver Island.

ROBERT BANK SUPERPORT

Just north of terminal is a bulk loading facility for shipment of coal from Fernie in S.E. B.C. to Japan. One mile trains carry 10,000 tons each. 100,000 ton boats carry it away at rate of 15,000,000 tons per year. Five men operate the facility.

ROBERTS BANK the shallow water across which the causeway crosses is part of the Fraser River delta. 20,000 Snow Geese winter here. Brant occur along the causeway from Feb. to May. Thousands of shore birds and many long legged Great Blue Herons stalk the shallows. People wading the shallows or digging in the muddy sand are gathering crabs or clams.

POINT ROBERTS The Canada-United States border is a few yards south of the terminal. The actual border is marked by a stone piling in the water and can be lined up with the shore marker as the ferry backs up past the rock breakwater. No, the shore marker is not the white marker bordered in red but the next one to the south. This is the longest unarmed border in the world which must attest to something!

FUR SEAL

ACTIVE PASS

This is one of the scenic highlights of all the routes to Vancouver Island.

Active Pass is named after the U.S. Revenue Schooner ACTIVE used to survey the 49th parallel in 1857. A captured smuggler told her crew he had received gold from Cariboo Indians and when crews reported this in San Francisco the Cariboo Gold Rush of 1858 was on.

CURRENTS 5-9 knot tide make it impossible for slower boats to navigate the pass except going with the current.

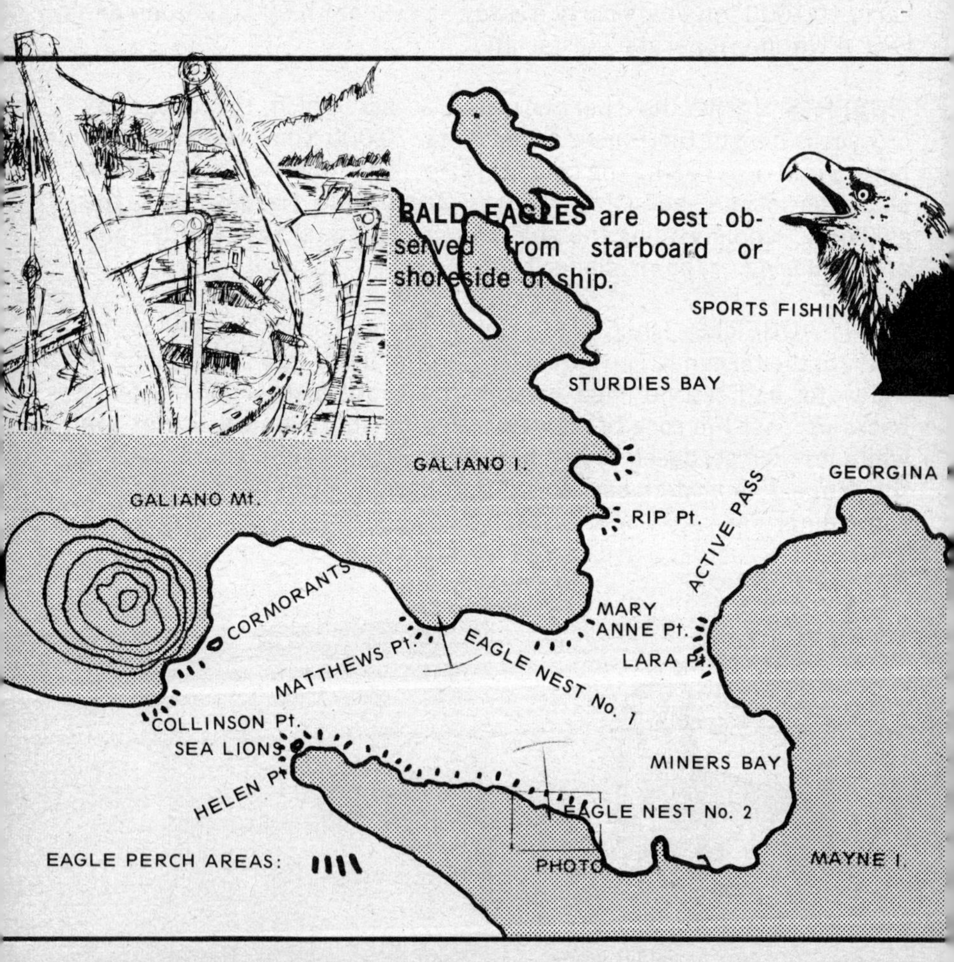

BALD EAGLES

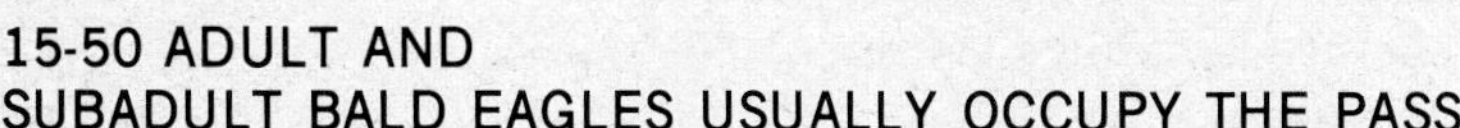

7 PAIRS NEST IN THE PASS

15-50 ADULT AND SUBADULT BALD EAGLES USUALLY OCCUPY THE PASS

NESTS Two nests are easily seen from ferry — both are marked with an arrow on map and can be seen from any point along arch of arrow. The photo at bottom, taken with a normal lens, shows nest No. 2 with large young standing in nest. Note nest is in crown of tree (see insert).

SWIMMING EAGLES On two occasions in Active Pass I have seen eagles swimming to shore dragging fish.

FLYING EAGLES often circle over ferry looking for fish churned up by vessel. Soaring eagles can often be seen taking advantage of up drafts over windward facing cliffs. Look for tiny specks high over Galiano Mountain.

EAGLE REST AREAS The shoreline where eagles often perch is outlined with hatch marks.

ACTIVE PASS POINTS OF INTEREST [N to S]

GOSSIP ISLAND on the NW side of Pass entrance. One legend says indians called it this because they waited here for good weather before crossing Straits — while they waited, they 'gossiped'.

GOSSIP SHOAL has bell buoy marking NW entrance.

GEORGINA POINT LIGHT is at NW end of Mayne Is. FL 9sec. 55ft. 12M. Can you interpret? page 9! In 1881 a settler found an English penny dated 1784 — possibly left here in 1792 by Capt. Vancouver when he first went ashore in the Islands.

STURDIES BAY Small retirement centre. Why do people live here? According to VICTORIAN columnist Ed Gould "Because they are not allowed to live anywhere else". Ouch!!!!

MINERS BAY on the W. end of Mayne Island has recently been invaded by land speculators. A result of the slick land subdivision schemes is that on weekends the 'beer and skittles crowd' toting 6 paks disgorge from the ferry singing with a slight lisp "The QUEEN of VICTORIA is a f a i r y". Long time Gulf Islanders — and they are a separate lot — are trying to curb land development to preserve the islands beauty, tranquility and sanity.

CAMERAS READY! **MARY ANNE LIGHT:** FL 30ft. 3M. The ferries usually meet rounding this point.

INDIAN VILLAGE A few cabins tucked in the bay on Helen Point are all that remain of a once flourishing summer fish camp owned by the Cowichan (Indian sweater fame) Indian Band of Duncan. Simon Fraser Univ. Archaeologists recently unearthed evidence that this site was occupied 4300 years ago — the oldest known lived in area in the Gulf Islands.

HELEN POINT Watch for SEA LIONS in bay on point beside marker light. Eagles usually in tall trees.

TRINCOMALI CHANNEL is named after the sailing frigate H.M.S. TRINCOMALII. She was built in Bombay in 1817 and sailed several times to this area. She was still afloat in 1968 as a holiday training ship Portsmouth Harbour.

NORTH PENDER ISLAND to the east is a retirement and tourist island that has successfully managed to miss the hustle-bustle. The smaller inter-island ferries serve the Otter Bay community on the north-west end

BEAVER POINT (opposite) is typical of the dry rocky outcroppings found in the Gulf Island area. Area is now a Provincial Park which offers several interesting beaches.

SALTSPRING ISLAND The rumor is not true that it was named by the Spaniard who found 'good water' but wanted to reserve it for themselves so sneakily named it Saltspring. It was actually named by the H.B.C. officers who found salt springs on the island.

BAYNE PEAK on Saltspring Island to north-west is a tremendous area for soaring hawks, and eagles. On any windy day from spring to fall Peregrine Falcons, Bald Eagles, Turkey Vultures, Red-tail Hawks and Cooper, Sharp-shinned, and Gos Hawks can be seen playing on the updrafts. (2030 feet)

PORTLAND ISLAND In the late '50's it was proposed to rename this island 'Princess Margaret Island' - The government had given the island to her and she was 'supposed' to donate it back to the people of the province. However, after and embarrassing wait the government had to ask her for the island back. The name remained unchanged!

KNAPP ISLAND on the east is a small privately owned island which housed a Bald Eagle nest. While the nest is not visible from the ferry the adult eagles are usually visible silhouetted in the tree tops.

REEF KNOT

BOWLINE

CLOVE HITCH

TWO HALF HITCHES

MAKING FAST TO A CLEAT

SHEEPSHANK

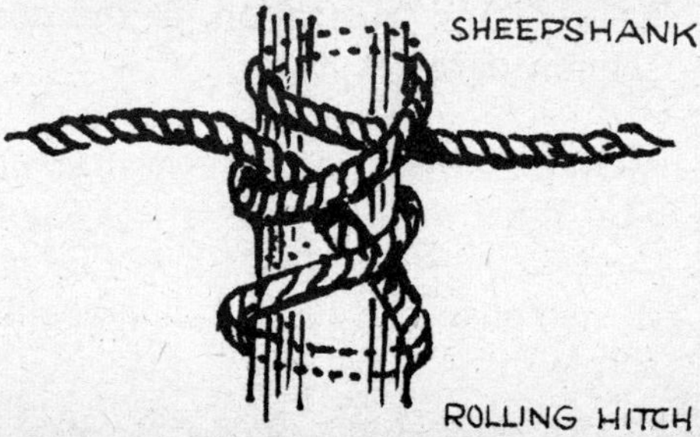

ROLLING HITCH

HORSESHOE BAY to DEPARTURE BAY [Nanaimo]

B.C. Ferries year round
Vessels: QUEENS of: TSAWWASSEN, NEW WESTMINSTER, BUR-
NABY and NANAIMO.

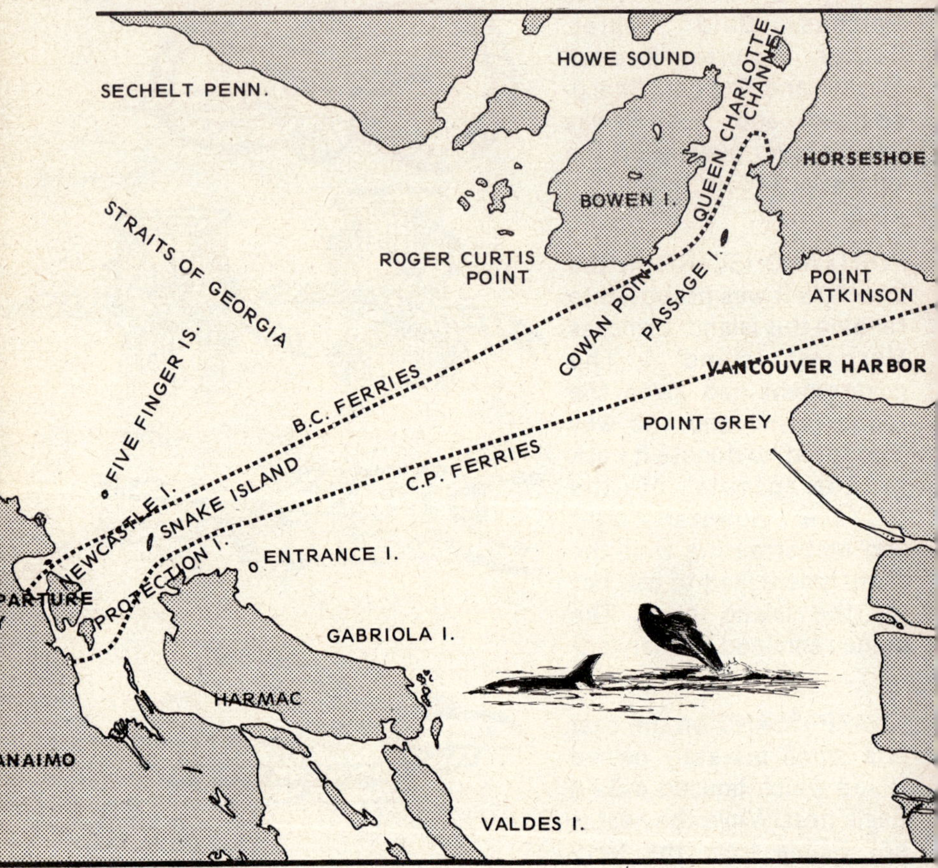

HORSESHOE BAY TERMINAL is one of the busiest terminals in North America with a ferry coming or going every 10 minutes. These include the Bowen Island and Sechelt ferries. In addition several thousand pleasure boats spread out from the harbor for fish, fun, frolic — and frustration for the docking ferry captains. The famous salmon derby is in August.

HOWE SOUND was named after Lord Howe in honor of his victory over the French in 1794 at the 'Glorious First of June' battle. In fact Capt. Richards of HMS PLUMPER who surveyed this region in 1858-61 named all the surrounding peaks and points after the officers and ships.

QUEEN CHARLOTTE CHANNEL after Howe's vessel. It leads north to the great peaks of Garibaldi Park.

BOWEN ISLAND, after the vessels master, is a resort and retirement centre.

SQUAMISH, is not only the name of a community at the head of Howe Sound just north of Woodfibre and Britannia Beach, but it is the name of a WIND that blows down the sound during periods of low pressure.

POINT ATKINSON LIGHT (Gp Fl(2) 5 sec. 108 16M ???? see page 5) was commissioned in 1875 and marks the northern entrance to Vancouver Harbor.

HORSESHOE BAY

STRAIT OF GEORGIA is the main sea lane to Alaska. There is open water here for 20 miles so if it blows and you haven't got your sea legs, or better your sea stomach, then I suggest that you find a window seat where you can watch the horizon and breath deeply. Most likely the crossing will be calm and now is a good time to find the dining room or cafeteria which offer superb food at reasonable prices. This is a great way to watch for passing traffic or WHALES.

GREY WHALE

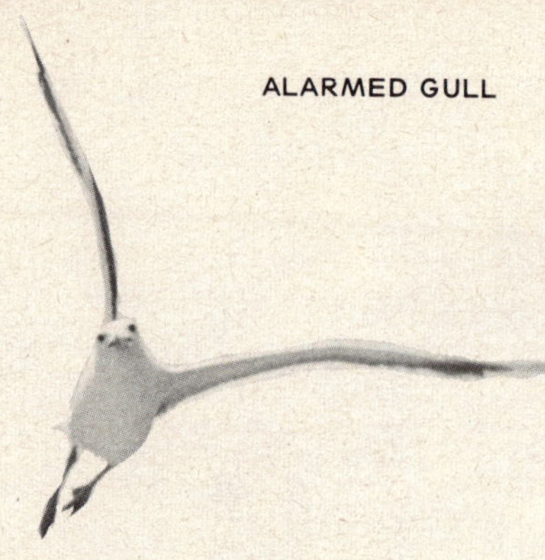

ALARMED GULL

SNAKE ISLAND on the south is a breeding colony for GLAUCOUS-WINGED GULLS and snakes.

NANAIMO HARBOR ENTRANCE where the C.P. Ferries dock is approached south of Snake Island.

BALD EAGLES: look on point.

NEWCASTLE ISLAND at south entrance to Departure Bay was site for Nanaimo's first coal discovery. Underground shafts connect the island with Vancouver Island. Nanaimo city is 100 years old in 1974.

KANAKA BAY at the northeast corner of Newcastle Island was named in honor of the Hawaiian Islanders brought here by the Hudson Bay Company as sheep herders even before THE BAY established a post in Hawaii in 1834. They are the blood stock of many of our pioneering families.

PACIFIC MURRE

SPORTS FISHING

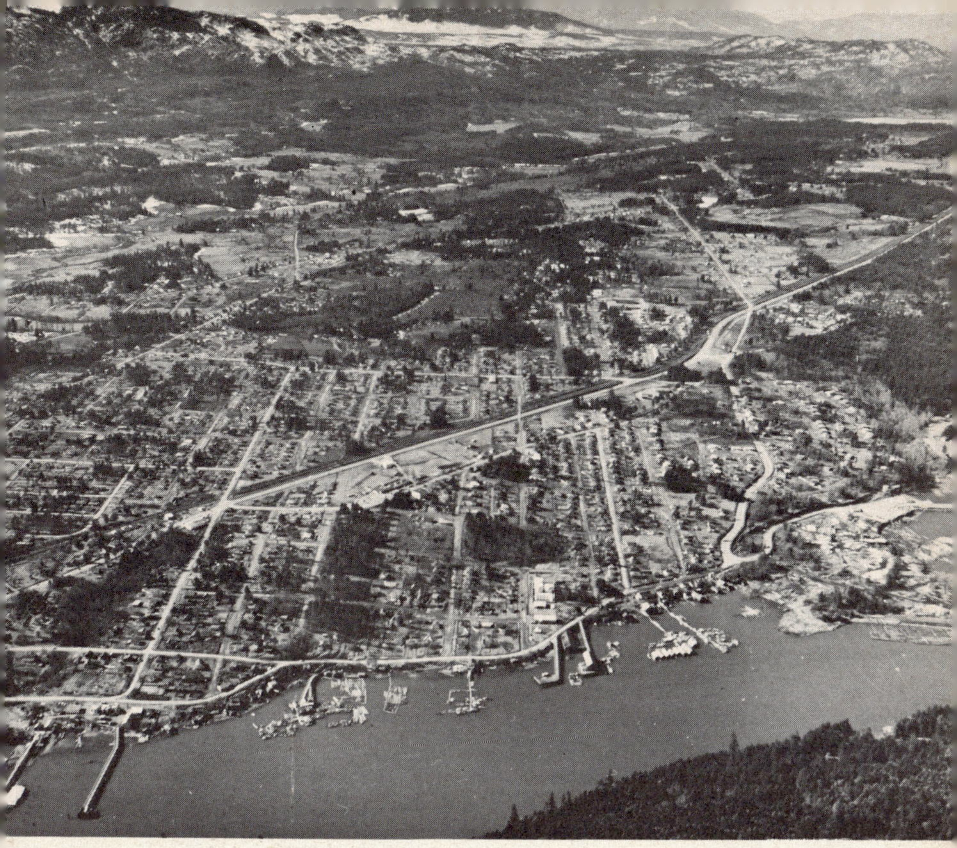

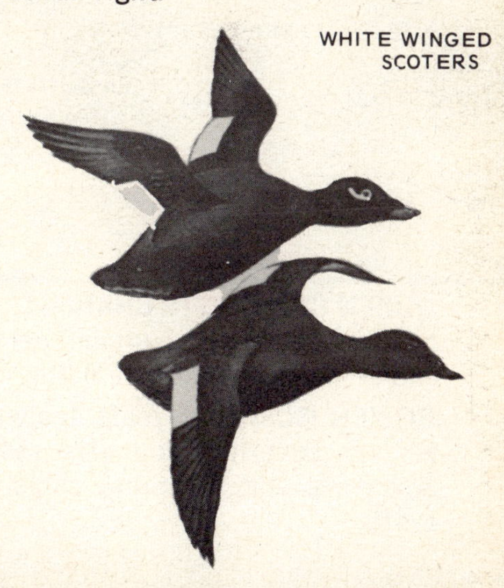

NANAIMO and its northern port Departure Bay are considered the Gateway to Vancouver Island. In the photo (above) one sees the foothills lightly touched with snow and Mount Hooper to right of centre. Nanaimo city centre is off photo to left. Newcastle Island is in foreground. B.C. Ferry terminal is at far right.

NANAIMO BIOLOGICAL STATION OPERATED by the Federal Fisheries Department (below) for studying salmon, herring, whales, etc., perches on the north side of the bay behind Jessie Island.

WHITE WINGED SCOTERS

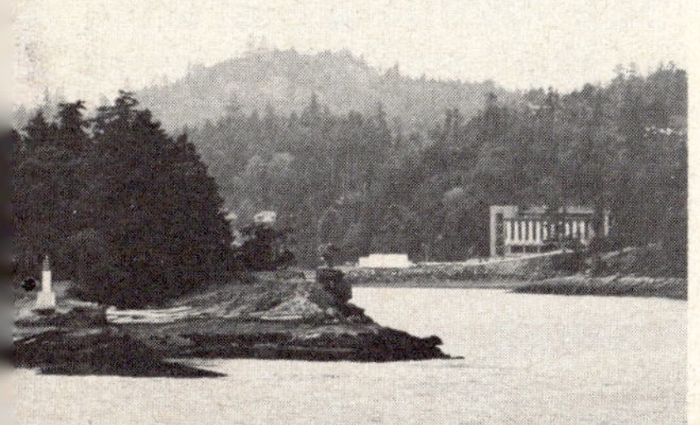

HORSHOE BAY to COMOX via POWELL RIVER

This is a year round service that requires three separate ferry rides and 70 miles of very scenic driving. This trip can be completed in a day but small fishing communities and side roads beg a longer look.

Vessels:

HORSESHOE BAY to LANGDALE B.C. Ferries.
 SUNSHINE COAST QUEEN and LANGDALE QUEEN

EARLS COVE to SALTERY BAY, B. C. Ferries
 POWELL RIVER QUEEN and BOWEN QUEEN

POWELL RIVER to COMOX
 COMOX QUEEN and QUEEN of the ISLANDS

QUEEN CHARLOTTE CHANNEL and HOWE SOUND and most of the points and nearby mountains were named after Lord Howe's officers and ships of the French Battle of 1794.

BOWEN ISLAND 25 years ago was the great excursion playground for Vancouverites and was served by many of the old Union Steamship and CP cruise ships. Today the island is a retirement centre.

HUTT ISLAND Once around Hood Point and Bowen Island the rounded dome of this island is seen off the port bow.

KNOTT ISLAND or SOAMER HILL is the next very conspicuous bump rising just behind Langdale terminal.

KEATS Island on the south has one of the few open treeless pastures and the area is known as Corkys' Farm.

TWIN ISLANDS on the north are a likely area to spot bald eagles in the tall trees.

PORT MELLON is 7 miles north up Thornbrough Channel and was British Columbia's first pulp mill. It was established in 1908 by Canadian Forest Products.

Hunter of the reefs: Great Blue Heron ———▶

EARLS COVE to SALTERY BAY.

SKOOKUMCHUK NARROWS which in Chinook language means 'turbulent waters' lives up to its name. The water draining out of the 40 miles of Sechelt, Narrow and Salmon Inlets burble over the Sechelt Rapids at 12 knots.

NELSON ISLAND is named after Lord Nelson of the Battle of Trafalgar fame.

JERVIS INLET is generally considered the most picturesque waterway on the coast. It stretches 30 miles north to be met by Princess Louisa Inlet.

POWER LINES AND BEARS Two power cables cross the channel to Nelson Island. These are a terrible hazard to low flying aircraft. Note the balls hanging from cable as warning. The photo shows a Black Bear standing at base of girder. Deer, bear, and cougar do well in the logged off areas because of the plentiful supply of new succulent plants. The many salmon spawning rivers are a bonanza in the fall for the bears, eagles and gulls.

LOG BOOMS Both Jervis Inlet and Howe Sound areas are used to store logs until the Vancouver and Powell River mills are ready for them.

POWELL RIVER to COMOX

POWELL RIVER This is the epitome of a loyal company town. If you ask about the smell of the pulp mill you get a broad smile and 'Great eh- that's the smell of money'. ——➤

WARSHIP BREAKWATER The booming ground beside the mill is unique in that it is formed of sunken retired World War II transport ships - some of which were made of concrete. The hull of the 1891 3 masted schooner CHARLES R. WILSON retired here after a life as a lumber ship and codfisher.

TEXADA ISLAND with its iron and limestone quarries is considered the richest mineralized real estate in British Columbia.

VENANDA is the mining community seen to south of Powell River just before the grey strip mining area.

BLUBBER BAY is an old whaling base which comes into view as we round the end of Texada.

FORBIDDEN PLATEAU is dead ahead across the Straits of Georgia. The 6870 foot peak of Mt. Albert Edward is seen in background.

COMOX VALLEY The low land profile behind the dock and below the Plateau is B.C.'s largest agricultural area with over 16,000 acres of beef, milk and vegetable farming.

CHARLES R. WILSON

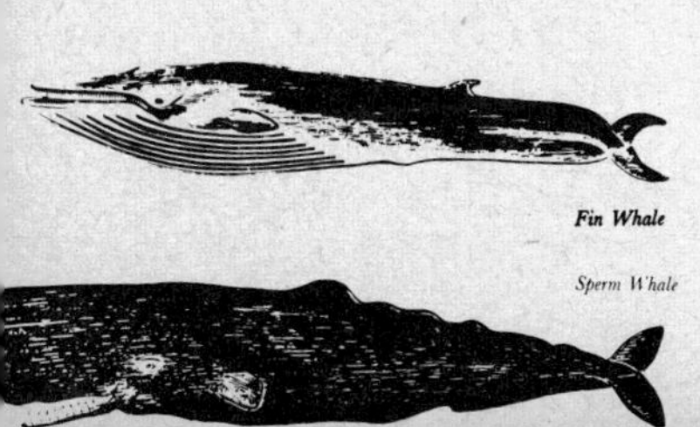

Fin Whale

Sperm Whale

PRINCE RUPERT to KELSEY BAY.

B. C. Ferries   year round
Vessel: QUEEN of PRINCE RUPERT

This route is more of an ocean cruise than a traditional ferry ride for it covers nearly 400 miles and takes 20 hours. The vessel is designed for open ocean travel. Little more than a few enticing comments can be given here for a whole booklet should be devoted to this trip.

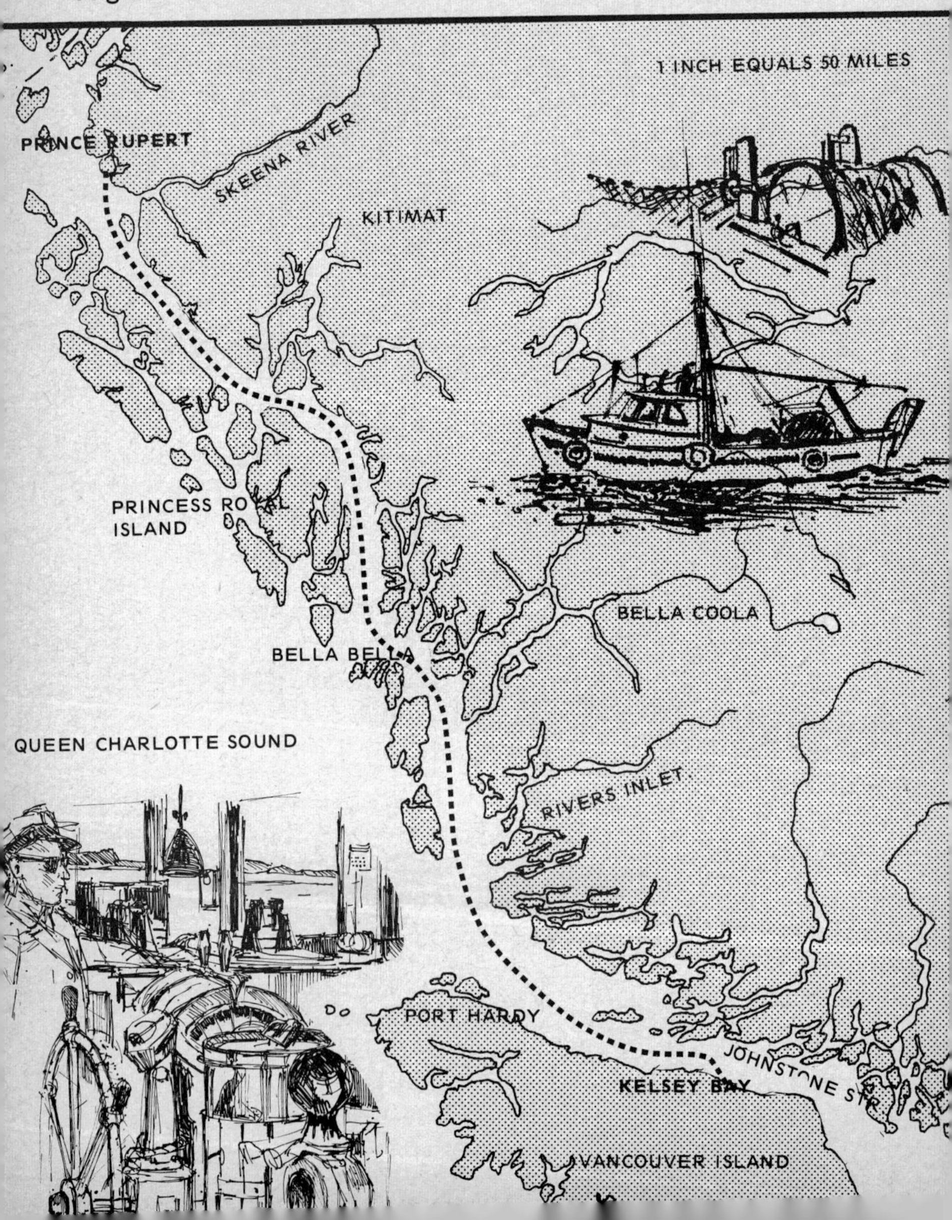

This coastal route can be thought of as the western highway to Alaska via the connecting Alaska Ferries out of Prince Rupert or Alaska via the new Stewart-Cassiar Highway or the Alaska Highway.
Some of the continents finest wilderness area lies along this route.

The sea off the Skeena River, Smith and Rivers Inlet, and Johnstone Strait are the most productive fish areas.

The mountain wilderness of Princess Royal Island houses the rare white Black Bears called Kermode Bears. The Indian called a pass just off route 'pour bouquos' or 'home of the hairy one' — in honor of the large number of Sasquatches seen gathering clams along the shore.

Great concentration of sea bird and gigantic Stellars Sea Lions are found on the isolated rocks. Johnstone Strait is hardly ever traversed without spotting the Killer Whales frolicking beside the boat. Bald Eagles fly in flocks.

STELLERS SEA LIONS

VANCOUVER to NANAIMO

C.P. Ferries   year round
Vessel: PRINCESS OF VANCOUVER

Extruded from the bowels of Vancouver the magnificence of her harbor should be enjoyed before partaking of the aging elegance of the PRINCESS'S superb dining lounge during the less interesting open Strait of Georgia crossing.

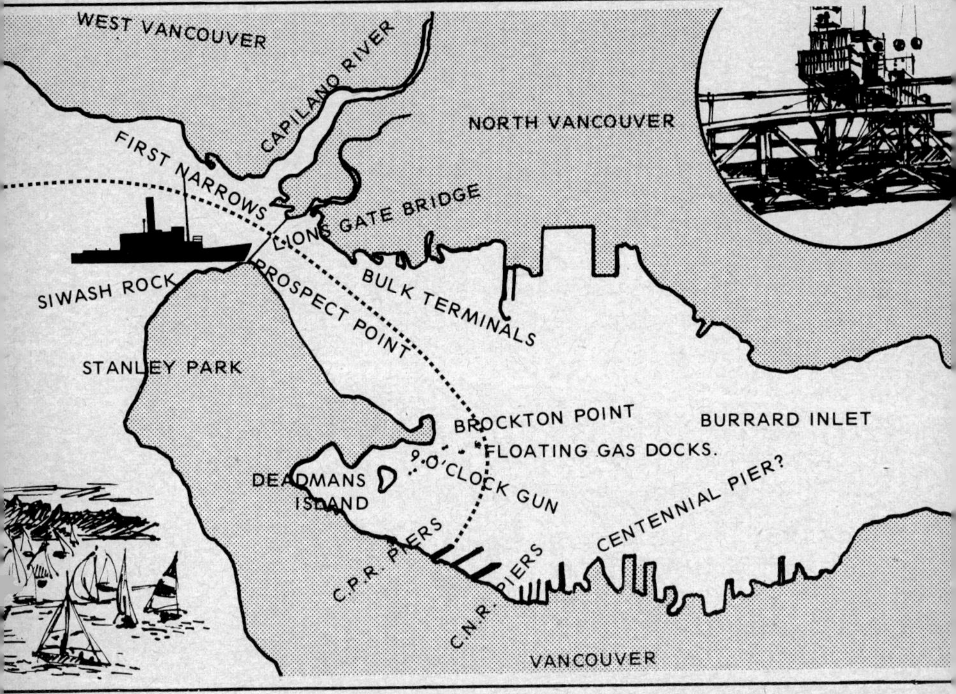

DEADMAN'S ISLAND joined by the causeway to Stanley Park now houses the HMCS Discovery. Formerly the tree burial area for the Capilano Indians and site where 200 warriors were sacrificed in return for release of captured women and children. In 1800 a whale oil refinery to light the lamps of Vancouver was located here.

9 O'CLOCK GUN has been fired daily since its placement on Hallelujah Point in 1894.

STANLEY PARK Established in 1886 this delightful park contains many Douglas Firs over 1000 years old. Named after Governor-General Lord Stanley. A pair of Bald Eagles nest in park.

NORTH SHORE BULK TERMINAL. The yellow piles are sulfur and the grey piles are potash for Japan.

LIONS GATE BRIDGE opened in 1938 and named for the two sphinx-like peaks standing guard over it to the north. The bridge is 209 feet high and sways eight feet in wind.

SIWASH ROCK According to one Indian legend the rock represents a wise and unselfish Indian leader who was turned into stone by the GREAT CHIEF ABOVE so that his good deed would be remembered by all.

PROSPECT POINT almost under Lions Gate Bridge is where the Hudson Bay Company's famous paddle steamer BEAVER grounded ending her 50 years of coastal service on a foggy 26 of July in 1888.

VANCOUVER HARBOR is the busiest harbor on the west coast and it is not uncommon to see 10 to 30 freighters anchored in the harbor waiting for loading. Thirty-five million tons pass through here annually.

WEST VANCOUVER The city of West Van perches picturesquely at the foot of Hollyburn Mountain. Looking eastward, North Vancouver is dominated by Grouse and Seymour Mountain.

SPANISH BANKS/POINT GREY The Fraser River sand piles up northeast of Point Grey to form Spanish Bank. It was here in 1792 that Capt. Vancouver met the Spanish explorers Galiano and Valdes.

HARLEQUIN DUCKS

GEORGIA STRAIT After passing point Atkinson Light the PRINCESS runs a parallel course with the B.C. Ferries going from Horseshoe Bay to Departure Bay — a northern suburb of Nanaimo. It is now time to partake of the elegant restaurant.

ENTRANCE ISLAND LIGHT on a barren rock to the south guides vessels into the Nanaimo Harbor.

SPORT FISHING is exceptionally good between Entrance Island and Snake Island to north, much to the consternation of the ferry boat captains who have to dodge the flotilla.

SNAKE ISLAND is named for both it's shape and occupants.

DEPARTURE BAY is seen to north of Nanaimo Harbor. The large square building is the Federal Fisheries Biological Station operated to study salmon, herring and whales.

HARMAC If you smelled rotten eggs out in the Straits don't blame the ferries cook — it was probably the sulfur emitted from this MacMillan Bloedel Pulp Mill. It is located just inside Gabriola Island to south.

BOOMING GROUNDS The pin cushion pilings between the pulp mill and the terminal are where log booms are tied up waiting delivery to Harmac or the lumber mill just south of ferry terminal.

PROTECTION AND NEWCASTLE ISLANDS as the name suggests were coal mining areas.

OLD BASTION Built in 1853 as a Hudson Bay fort and trading post, the BASTION commanded a view of the harbor approaches. Now it is a fine museum.

GALLOWS POINT (opposite page at bottom) was a favorite place for hanging villans. The site now hosts the Gallows Point Light House. A coal mine shaft connects the point with Nanaimo.

VANCOUVER — SWARTZ BAY

C.P. Ferry
vessel:

year round

CARRIER PRINCESS

This service is primarily designed for truck transport but the PRINCESS has fine lounges and restaurant facilities for the traveller wishing a direct downtown Vancouver service.

Since the route overlaps the Vancouver-Nanaimo (page 33) and Tsawwassen-Swartz Bay (page 15) routes this one is not separately described here.

SEATTLE to VICTORIA

C. P. Ferries   summer only
Vessel: PRINCESS MARGUERITE

With the stateroom organized, a drink under the belt in the lounge to relieve the pressures of overtowering Space Needles, crowded streets and insane freeways, the relaxed atmosphere of Ye Olde Victoria is already becoming a reality. As a farewell gesture lift your glass to West Point.

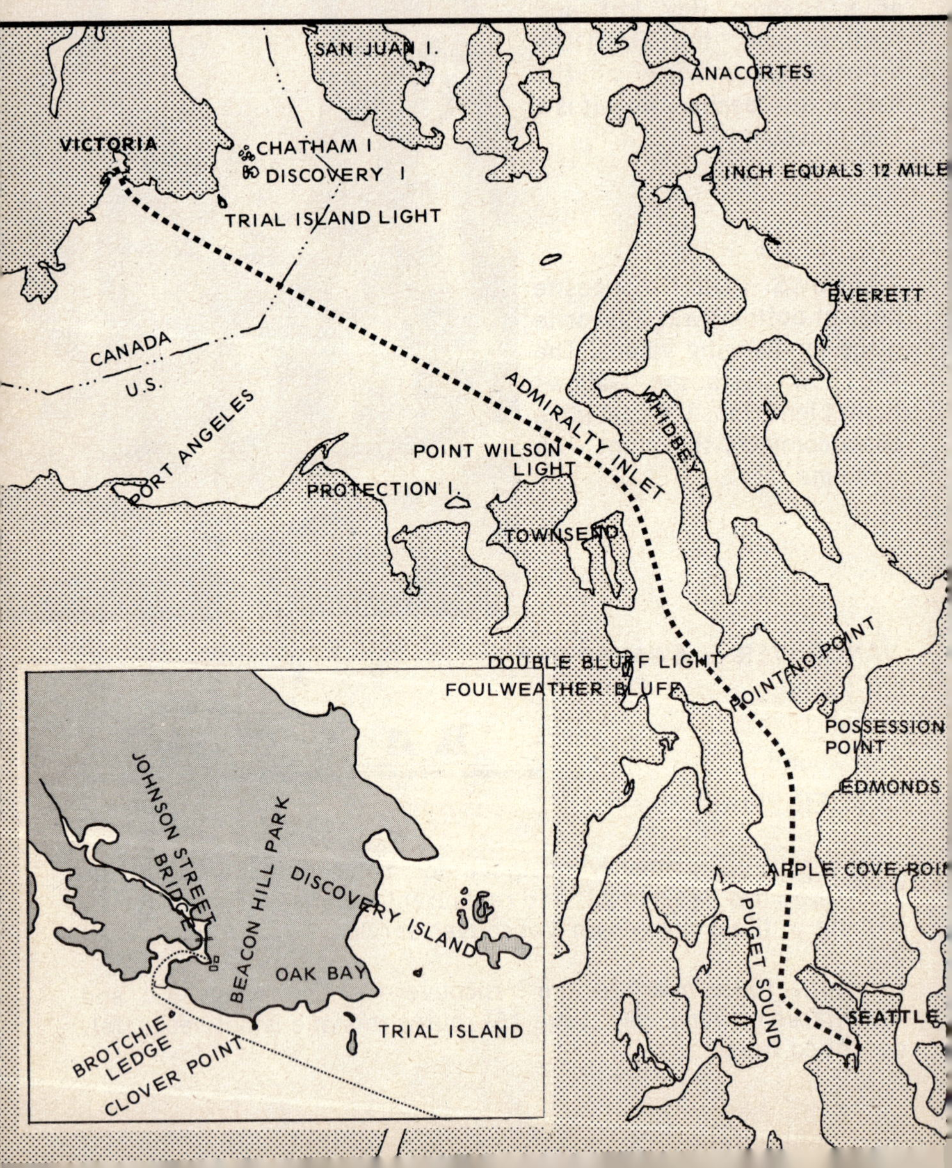

WEST POINT houses Seattle's Sewage Treatment Plant. Care must be taken to correctly spell the name of the adjacent Shilshole Bay which receives the polluted industrial drainage from Lakes Washington and Union.

PORT MADISON on the west is surrounded by Monroe and Jefferson Points honoring the 4th, 5th and 3rd U.S. Presidents respectively.

EDMONDS opposite on the east shore is an outer suburb of Seattle joined to Kingston in Appletree Cove by W.S. Ferries.

APPLE COVE POINT on west was named by Wilkes Expedition 1841 when they thought Dogwoods were apple trees.

WHIDBEY ISLAND and PUGET SOUND were named for Capt. Vancouver's two officers who did most of the initial exploration of this area.

POSSESSION POINT off the south end of Whidbey Island was named on June 4, 1792 by Captain Vancouver to celebrate King George III's birthday. He took all the land for England and named it 'New Georgia'.

POINT-NO-POINT is a great salmon fishing area. The PRINCESS VICTORIA collided here in 1914 with the SS ADMIRAL SAMPSON. The latter sank in 4 minutes. The Grand Lady of the fleet, PRINCESS VIC, put in 48 years on the coast before being stripped of her pride to become a hog fuel barge in 1951.

POINT-NO-POINT

DOUBLE BLUFF LIGHT F1 G 5sec. 60ft. 10M (see page 9) This is one of the Sounds most conspicuous land marks.

FOULWEATHER BLUFF As every commercial ship passes the SIERRA CHARLIE mark north of the Bluff it reports to Seattle Traffic Centre its position, direction and speed. Another similar marker off Port Angeles checks incoming traffic and plots progress on a computer.

ADMIRALTY INLET is not only a busy commercial traffic lane but is well frequented by small dark fast flying sea birds called RHINOCEROS AUKLETS which all breed on Protection Island past Port Townsend. The inlet was named by Capt. Vancouver for his governing board.

PORT TOWNSEND like most pulp mills towns is usually smelled before it is seen.

PROTECTION ISLAND houses one of few inside waters Rhinoceros Auklet colonies.

DISCOVERY AND CHATHAM ISLANDS were named after the two ships used by Capt. Vancouver in his round the world trip during which he stopped at Nootka in 1792 to supervise the terms of the 1790 Nootka convention which gave all Spanish claims to area to England. He then charted much of the inland waters from Seattle to Alaska.

TRIAL ISLAND LIGHT is to west on a barren rock and in front of Victoria's Oak Bay district. The trim red and white buildings are characteristic of the Canadian Dept. of Transport facilities.

BEACON HILL PARK named for two beacons which when lined up warned sailing vessels of the position of dangerous Brotchie Ledge at the harbor entrance.

BROTCHIE LEDGE has claimed many ships including the San Pedro which after six years slide into deep water. and is still explored by divers.

The C.P. Ferry often cuts inside this reef on route to Seattle affording a close look at the Dallas Road and Clover Point Lookout - some sewer outlet areas. This is a great birding area.

VICTORIA Below is a seagull's view of Victoria, one of the world's most charming cities. Here you'll find the world's tallest totem pole, and the ancient Craigdarroch Castle; here you may go sight-seeing in a horse-drawn Tally Ho cart, or watch horse racing at Sandown Park. Victoria is famous as the city of a thousand gardens — but perhaps best known as a corner of Olde England off the west coast of Canada.

ANACORTES TO SIDNEY

WASHINGTON STATE FERRIES - year round.
Vessels: EVERGREEN STATE and WALLA WALLA

HISTORY: Ahead lies one of the most exciting ferry rides in North America to the submerged mountain range known as the San Juan Islands.

Between 1774 and 1793 the Spaniards reigned supreme under explorers like Juan Perez, Hecata, Quadra, Lopez de Haro, and Francisco Eliza who named the islands. In 1792-93 Captain Vancouver came to accept the land in England's name following the Nootka Convention and explore the inside waters from Seattle to Alaska. The Hudson Bay Company quickly moved in to exploit the lucrative fur market and brought in the sheep and Hawaiian herders

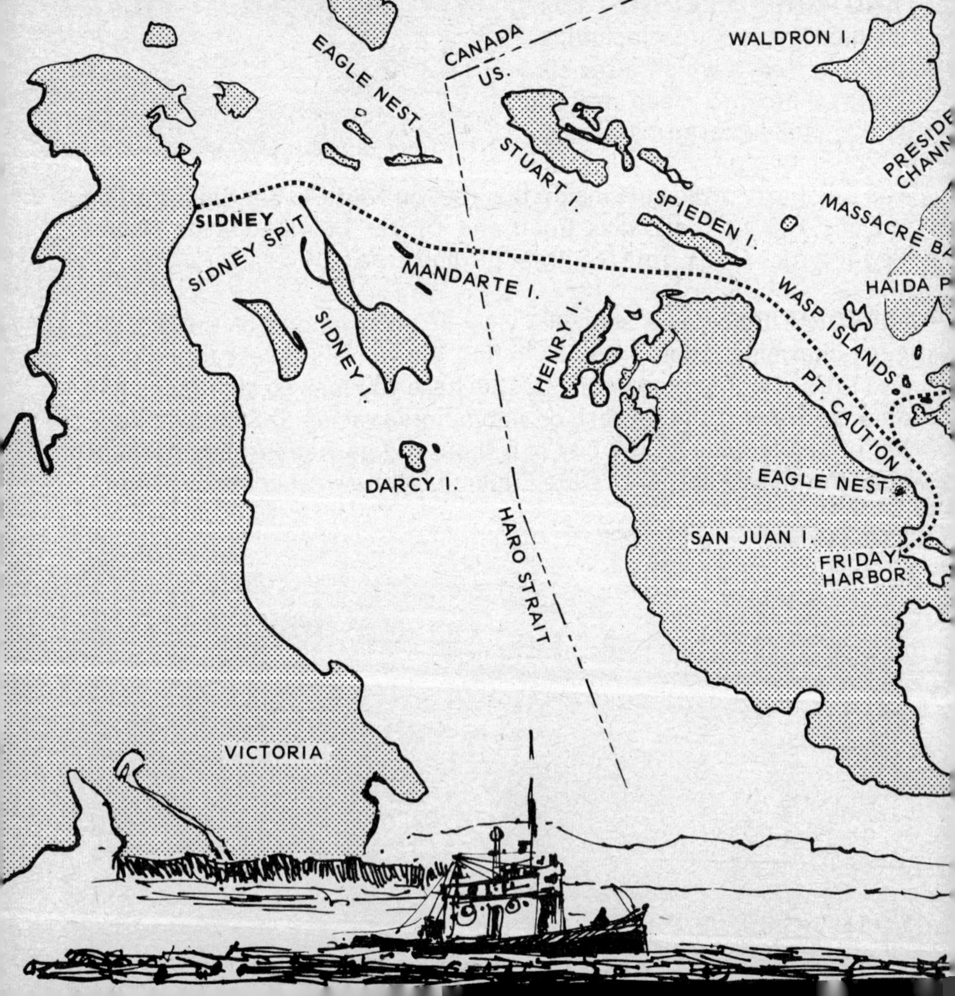

- the Kanakas - to further establish England's sovereignty. Escaping Negro slaves, homesteading Americans, disappointed 1858 Cariboo Gold seekers slowly populated the islands. But who owned them? The English or the American occupants??

PIG WAR: The H.B.C. manager on San Juan named Griffin had a pig that kept eating the garden of an American squatter named Cutler. The latter shot the pig. When British Officers arrived to arrest Cutler he hid. Other Americans raised a flag on July 4 and this attracted the passing U.S. Military who came ashore and under pretext of defending U.S. citizens against the Indians set up camp. The British immediately established a garrison at the north end of San Juan and a friendly truce persisted until in 1872 when Kaiser Wilhelm 1 of Germany arbitrated the disputed island in U.S. favor.

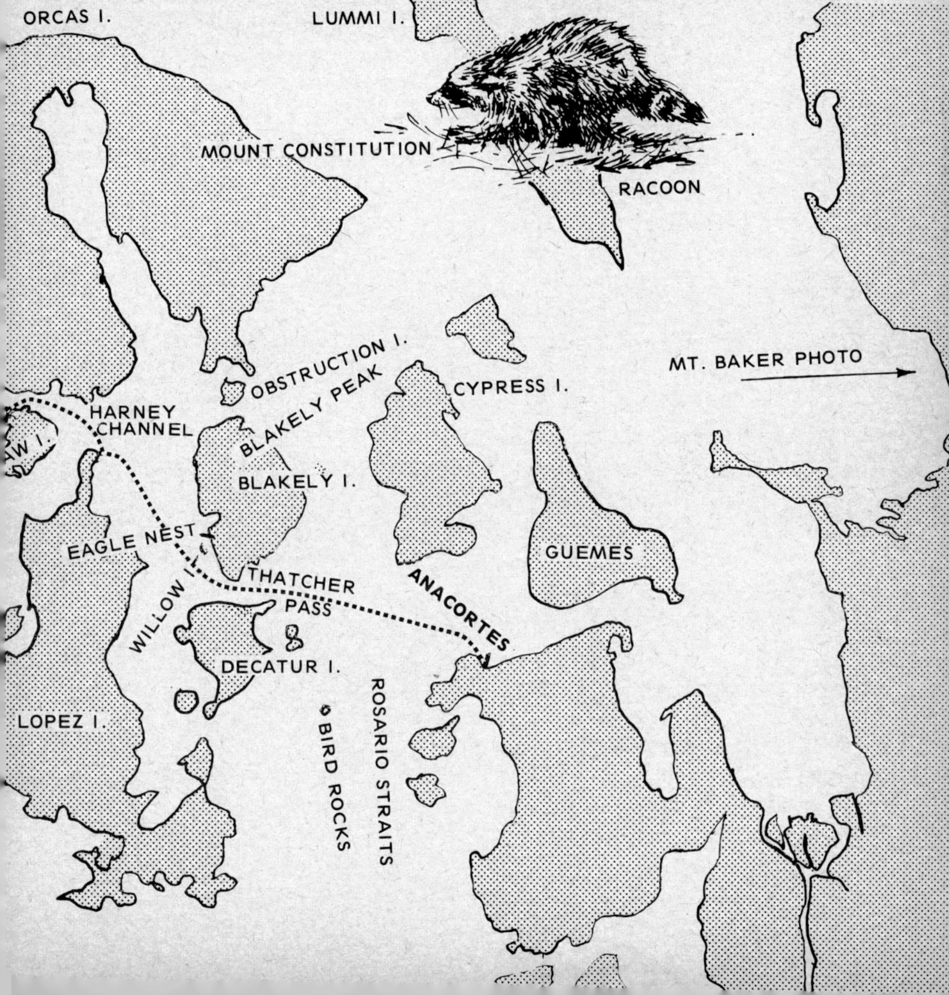

ROSARIO STRAIT This is the main deep water sea lane from Seattle to Vancouver and Alaska. If the wind whips up this stretch of open water this is a good place to test your 'sea legs' or seasick pills.

BIRD ROCKS to the south are occupied by several hundred nesting sea birds. The island is used as a bombing target by the U.S. Air Force pilots based at Whidbey Island.

TUFTED PUFFIN

BALD EAGLES This endangered species and United States National Emblem is commonly seen in this region - see page 13. Check the big trees along shoreline for the white head in Thatcher Pass.

BALD EAGLE NEST with adults in attendance from January to July, is located on Blakely Island just north of

Willow Island as a light brown spot two-thirds way up the hillside.

MOUNT CONSTITUTION to the north in Moran State Park on Orcas Island is the highest peak in the islands at nearly 2500 feet. and is topped by the Bellingham TV tower. The park was named after a poor New Yorker who became Seattle's mayor and retired in poor health to Orcas with one year to live. He lived another 40 years in the relaxed atmosphere and donated the Park.

LOPEZ ISLAND is a quiet farming and fishing area of 500 residents who pride themselves in having few roads, no industry and no payrolls. What audacity!

SHAW ISLAND is even worse - or perhaps that should be better - for these islanders won't permit any tourist facilities.

ENTERING THATCHER PASS FROM THE WEST. ———

YOU DON'T SAY! When a resident Negro San Juan Islander was asked by a tourist who were the first white settlers in the islands he would proudly reply: "Ma family wus d'first white people heer."

MOUNT BAKER is magnificently beautiful from Harney Channel looking eastward. The 10,778 foot snow capped peak is framed between Obstruction Island and Blakely Peak. The mountain was named by Capt. Vancouver in 1792.

ORCAS ISLAND is the fruit bowl of the northwest. It is dominated by Mt. Constitution and tourist facilities.

MASSACRE BAY west of Orcas and at the head of West Sound with its Skull Bay and Haida Point attests to earlier wild times when the local Coast Salish Indians were attacked by the northern tribes.

WASP PASSAGE was named for the U.S. Sloop-of-War which surveyed area. Check shore for eagles.

WASP ISLANDS were a famed hide-out area for pirates, rum runners, opium and Chinese laboror smugglers. Wool smuggled from Canada where it was half price earned the San Juan sheep the distinction of producing more wool per animal than any sheep in any other part of the world.

SEA OTTER

MUSSELS opposite, abound on nearby rocks and pilings and are all edible.

SAN JUAN ISLAND is famed for having the fastest breeding rabbits in the world. The area is a great farming, fishing and tourist area.

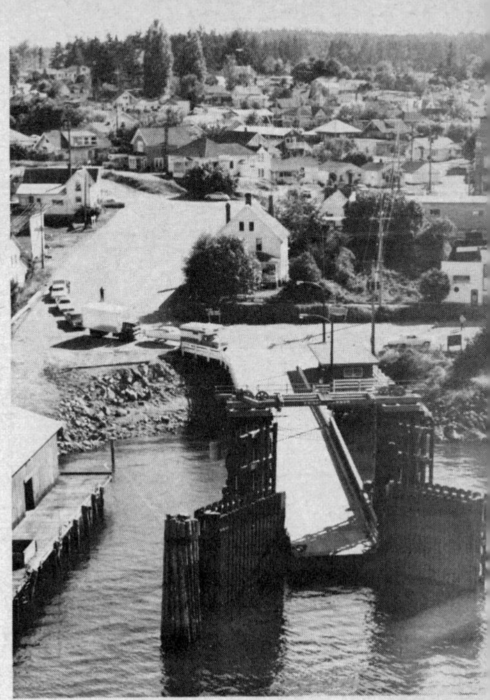

FRIDAY HARBOR After passing the EAGLE NEST on Point Caution you enter harbor where buildings on the north belong to famous Washington Institute of Oceanography.

FISH AND PEA Just S.E. of the terminal the old tin buildings are the remains of the once flourishing fish and pea cannery. The red building adjacent to the dock is still used to dry out nets.

SPIEDEN ISLAND with its long barren brown slope is a hunting resort where zoo and captive raised animals are released for "sportsman" to kill.

MANDARTE ISLAND is a sea bird nesting rookery that in the past was a valuable egg collecting area for the Indians. Now the island is leased to the University of British Columbia for their bird studies. The nude people roaming the island are sun loving biologists. Binoculars down!

SIDNEY SPIT on the south is first B.C. Marine Park. It hosts thousands of pleasure boats to enjoy its beaches, fishing and crabs.

SIDNEY VILLAGE is a quiet retirement centre just north of the terminal which has a fish wharf at the end of Main Street that offers fresh fillets and crabs for your lunch.

THE FIVE SPECIES OF PACIFIC SALMON ARE ILLUSTRATED TO LEFT.

CHINOOK

Lightly spotted on blue-green back, chinooks live from five to seven years, weigh up to 120 pounds. They are most famous game salmon, are sold commercially mainly in fresh or frozen state.

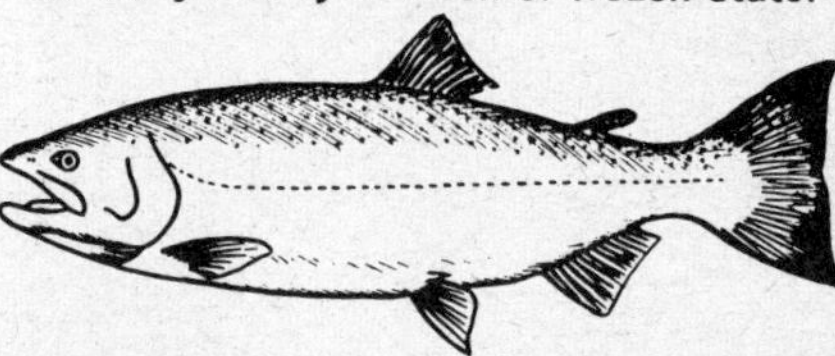

COHO

Bright silver in color, coho live three years, weigh up to 15 pounds. A popular sport fish, they are sold commercially fresh. frozen, canned and smoked.

SOCKEYE

Blue-tinged silver in color, sockeye live four to five years, weigh up to seven pounds. Slimmest and most streamlined of the species, they are used solely for canning.

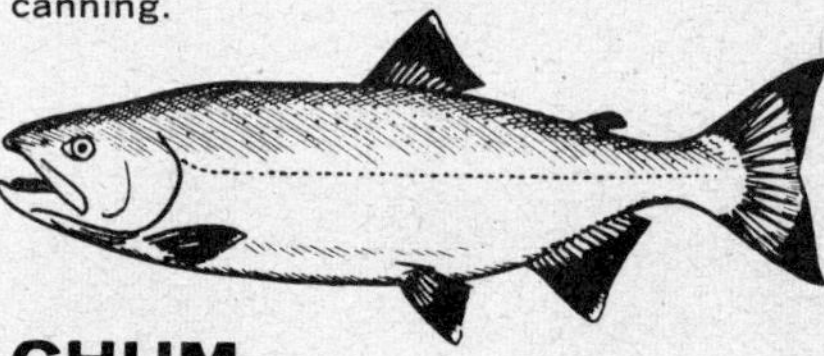

CHUM

Resembling sockeye, chums have black specks over their silvery sides, and faint grid-like bars. Living three to five years, they weigh up to 10 pounds, are used only for canning.

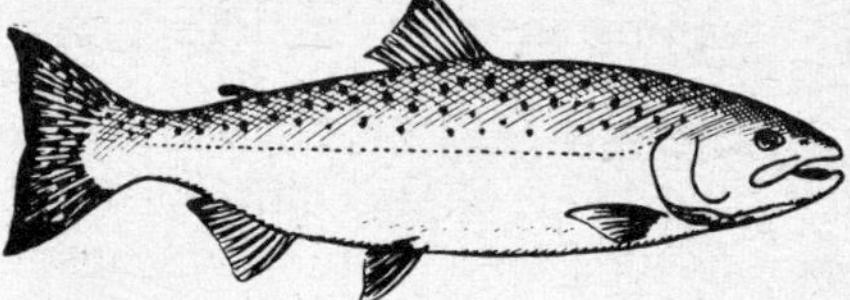

PINK

Living only two years, pinks are smallest of Pacific salmon, weighing up to five pounds. They have heavily-spotted backs over silver bodies, and are also used only for canning.

PORT ANGELES TO VICTORIA

Black Ball Ferries Year round
Vessel: COHO

C.P. Ferries Summer only
Vessel: PRINCESS MARGUERITE

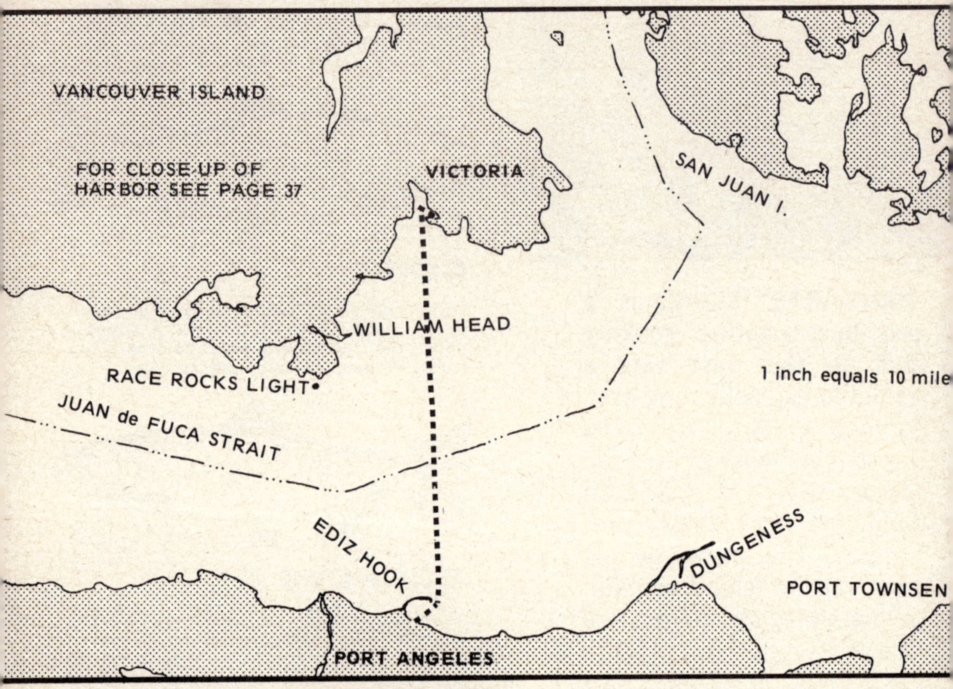

PULP MILLS: ITT RAYONIER pulp mill is visible east of CPR and Black Ball terminals and it specializes in producing most of the North American supply of acetate backing used in film manufacture.

PENPLY is the first mill west of Black Ball terminal, with log booms waiting in front; it produces plywood.

CROWN ZELLERBACH'S huge pulp and paper mill is seen spewing smelly smoke at base of Ediz Hook. Much of the pulp for this mill comes from the British Columbia forests.

PORT ANGELES HARBOR situated on Juan de Fuca Strait is well protected from the open ocean swells by a large sand bar - Ediz Hook. The Coast Pilots board incoming frieghters here to help them navigate the inside waters.

EDIZ HOOK Originally a summer Indian encampment, the sand spit now houses a public park, boat launching ramp and the United States Coast Guard Air-Sea Rescue Base. The small pleasure boats off the spit are fishing for salmon.

JUAN DE FUCA STRAITS is the southern entrance to the great Inland Passage. Oceanic sea birds often enter here in bad weather. Shearwaters, Petrels.

RACE ROCKS LIGHT 105 foot tower seen to west off south end of Vancouver Island was built with stone brought from England.

WILLIAM HEAD is the next point towards Victoria and is named after Queen Victoria's husband — a fitting introduction to Ye Olde Victoria.

VICTORIA HARBOR breakwater protects the outer Ogden Point docks. The inner harbor with it's magnificent Empress Hotel and Parliament Buildings (see page 40) near terminal is separated from main industrial harbor by the Johnson Street Bridge here preparing for passage of the Oceanographic vessel VECTOR.

ROUTE 1: Vancouver (Tsawwassen) to Victoria (Swartz Bay)
(British Columbia Ferries, 816 Wharf Street, Victoria, British Columbia).
Crossing time: 1 hour 40 minutes.

Winter, Spring, and Fall (January 8 to April 18) (recommences September 24):
Every two hours, 7 a.m. to 9 p.m.
Monday, Tuesday, Wednesday, Thursday, Saturday, and Sunday — additional sailings.
Friday — every hour, 7 a.m. to 10 p.m.

Summer (April 19 to September 23):
Every hour, 7 a.m. to 10 p.m.

Rates	One Way
Passengers	$2.00
Automobiles	$5.00

Children, 5 through 11: Half fare.
Vertical clearance, 14 feet 8 inches.
No reservations.
Trailer rates: Same as Route 1.

Reduced Passenger Fare

Tuesdays, Wednesday, Thursdays only except holidays. (Not applicable to drivers of recreational vehicles, pickups, or panels.)

ROUTE 2: Vancouver (Horseshoe Bay) to Nanaimo (Departure Bay) (British Columbia Ferries, 816 Wharf Street, Victoria, British Columbia).
Crossing time: 1 hour 50 minutes.

Winter (January 8 to April 18) (recommences September 24 to December 31):
Every 2 hours 15 minutes, 6.15 a.m. to 10 p.m.
Monday, Tuesday, Wednesday, Thursday, Saturday, Sunday — additional sailings.
Friday —
Every 2 hours 15 minutes (6.15 a.m. to 10 p.m.)
Every 2 hours 15 minutes (7.15 a.m. to 11 p.m.).

Spring and Fall (April 19 to June 28) (recommences September 5 to September 23):
Every 2 hours 15 minutes (6.15 a.m. to 10 p.m.).
Every 2 hours 15 minutes (7.15 a.m. to 11 p.m.).

Summer (June 20 to September 4):
Every 2 hours 30 minutes (6 a.m. to 11:30 p.m.).
Every 2 hours 30 minutes (7 a.m. to 12:30 a.m.).

Rates	One Way
Passengers	$2.00
Automobiles	5.00

Children, 5 through 11: Half fare.
Vertical clearance, 14 feet 8 inches.
No reservations.
Trailer rates: Up to 8 feet, $3.30; 8 feet to 18 feet, $5; over 18 feet, 64 cents per foot.

Reduced Passenger Fare

Tuesdays, Wednesdays, Thursdays, only, except holidays. (Not applicable to drivers of recreational vehicles, pickups, or panels).

ROUTE 3: Horseshoe Bay to Comox (British Columbia Ferries and Dept. of Highways).

Horseshoe Bay:
Winter: Leave Horseshoe Bay approximately every 1 - 1½ hours
Summer: Leave Horseshoe Bay approximately every hour.

Earls Cove:
Winter and summer:
Leave Earls Cove approximately every 2 hours.

Powell River:
Winter and Summer:
Leave Comox (Little River) 7:30 a.m., 11:15 a.m., 3:00 p.m., 7:00 p.m.
Leave Powell River 9:15 a.m., 1:00 p.m., 5:10 p.m., 8:45 p.m.
Extra sailings: daily during summer season (mid June to mid October 1973).
Phone Courtenay 334-4432.

Rates

Both ferries under one ticket.

Passengers	adult $2.00
	children $1.00
automobiles & pickups	6.00
trucks & trailers	6.00
	+ .65 / ft. over 18'

No reservations.

Rates

	One Way
Passengers	$2.00
Automobiles and pickup trucks	5.00

No reservations.
Trucks and trailers: $3.50 per 9 feet of length.

ROUTE 4: Kelsey Bay to Prince Rupert (British Columbia Ferries, Tsawwassen, Delta, British Columbia).
Sailing time: 20 hours; 330 miles.

Winter (January 1 to May 5) (September 25 to December 30):
Layover, May 6 at Kelsey Bay.
North-bound from Kelsey Bay every Tuesday and Thursday, leave 1:30 p.m.
South-bound from Prince Rupert every Wednesday and Saturday, leave 12:30 p.m.

Summer (May 7 to September 23):
Layover, September 24 at Kelsey Bay.
North-bound from Kelsey Bay every other day, May 7 to September 22, leave at 1:30 p.m.
South-bound from Prince Rupert every other day, May 8 to September 23, leave 12:30 p.m.

Rates

Passengers:

One way	$30.00

Children, 5 to 11 yrs.: Half fare.
10 per cent reduction on return passenger fares. Meals not included.
Automobiles (including driver):

One way	$60.00
Return fare	114.00

Mobile homes and campers up to 20 feet (including driver)   75.00
Return fare   144.00
Passenger-vehicle trailers, utility trailers, boat trailers: $3.60 per foot.
Reservations recommended.
Staterooms available at additional charge.
(Inquire re autumn to spring reductions.)